BOOK CLUB IN A BOX

Bookclub-in-a-Box presents the discussion companion for Alan Bennett's novel
The Uncommon Reader

Published by Faber and Faber,
Profile Books, London, 2007.
Originally published, London Review of Books, 2006.
ISBN: 978-1-84668-049-6

Quotations used in this guide have been taken from the text of the paperback edition of **The Uncommon Reader**. All information taken from other sources is acknowledged.

This discussion companion for **The Uncommon Reader** has been prepared and written by Marilyn Herbert, originator of Bookclub-in-a-Box. Marilyn Herbert. B.Ed., is a teacher, librarian, speaker and writer. Bookclub-in-a-Box is a unique guide to current fiction and classic literature intended for book club discussions, educational study seminars, and personal pleasure.

This guide was co-written by Erin Balser. For more information about the Bookclub-in-a-Box team, visit our website.

Bookclub-in-a-Box discussion companion for People of the Book

ISBN 10: 1-897082-57-6
ISBN 13: 978-1897082577

This guide reflects the perspective of the Bookclub-in-a-Box team and is the sole property of Bookclub-in-a-box.

©2009 - MR - BOOKCLUB-IN-A-BOX

Unauthorized reproduction of this book or its contents for republication in whole or in part is strictly prohibited.

CONTACT INFORMATION: SEE BACK COVER.

BOOKCLUB-IN-A-BOX
Alan Bennett's The Uncommon Reader

READERS AND LEADERS GUIDE 2

INTRODUCTION

    Novel Quickline 7

    Keys to the Novel 8

    Author Information 9

    Background Information . . .12

CHARACTERIZATION

    The Queen 19

    Sir Kevin Scatchard 22

    Norman Seakins 24

    The Prime Minister 25

    Sir Claude Pollington 26

FOCUS POINTS / THEMES

    The Power of Reading 29

    The Reader 32

    The Writer 33

    Borrowing 34

    Private Lives, Public Lives . .35

    The Monarchy 36

WRITING STYLE/STRUCTURE

    The Novel's Framework . . .42

    Writing Style 43

    Humor and Satire 44

LAST THOUGHTS

    Fictionalizing the Queen . . .49

    The Lady in the Van 50

    Uncommon Readers 51

    Bennett's Works 56

    The Queen's Reading List . .61

    Suggested Beginnings 66

FROM THE NOVEL (QUOTES) . . .71

ACKNOWLEDGEMENTS 79

BOOKCLUB-IN-A-BOX

Readers and Leaders Guide

Each Bookclub-in-a-Box guide is clearly and effectively organized to give you information and ideas for a lively discussion, as well as to present the major highlights of the novel. The format, with a Table of Contents, allows you to pick and choose the specific points you wish to talk about. It does not have to be used in any prescribed order. In fact, it is meant to support, not determine, your discussion.

You Choose What to Use.

You may find that some information is repeated in more than one section and may be cross-referenced so as to provide insight on the same idea from different angles.

The guide is formatted to give you extra space to make your own notes.

How to Begin

Relax and look forward to enjoying your Bookclub.

With Bookclub-in-a-Box as your behind the scenes support, there is little for you to do in the way of preparation.

Some readers like to review the guide after reading the novel; some before. Either way, the guide is all you will need as a companion for your discussion. You may find that the guide's interpretation, information, and background have sparked other ideas not included.

Having read the novel and armed with Bookclub-in-a-Box, you will be well prepared to lead or guide or listen to the discussion at hand.

Lastly, if you need some more 'hands-on' support, feel free to contact us. (See Contact Information)

What to Look For

Each Bookclub-in-a-Box guide is divided into easy-to-use sections, which include points on characters, themes, writing style and structure, literary or historical background, author information, and other pertinent features unique to the novel being discussed. These may vary slightly from guide to guide.

INTERPRETATION OF EACH NOVEL REFLECTS THE PERSPECTIVE OF THE BOOKCLUB-IN-A-BOX TEAM.

Do We Need to Agree?
THE ANSWER TO THIS QUESTION IS NO.

If we have sparked a discussion or a debate on certain points, then we are happy. We invite you to share your group's alternative findings and experiences with us. You can respond on-line at our website or contact us through our Contact Information. We would love to hear from you.

Discussion Starters

There are as many ways to begin a Bookclub discussion as there are members in your group. If you are an experienced group, you will already have your favorite ways to begin. If you are a newly formed group or a group looking for new ideas, here are some suggestions.

Ask for people's impressions of the novel. (This will give you some idea about which parts of the unit to focus on.)

- Identify a favorite or major character.
- Identify a favorite or major idea.
- Begin with a powerful or pertinent quote. (not necessarily from the novel)
- Discuss the historical information of the novel. (not applicable to all novels)
- If this author is familiar to the group, discuss the range of his/her work and where this novel stands in that range.
- Use the discussion topics and questions in the Bookclub-in-a-Box guide.

If you have further suggestions for discussion starters, be sure to share them with us and we will share them with others.

Above All, Enjoy Yourselves

INTRODUCTION

Novel Quickline

Keys to the Novel

Author Information

Background Information

INTRODUCTION

Novel Quickline

As unlikely as it might seem, the Queen could be the ultimate cocktail party guest or trivia player. She has a tremendous range of knowledge. She knows how to make interested, but not intimate conversation that involves small talk, but not debate. She is a model royal, taking to her public duties with pride and care.

But the monarchy is turned upside down when the Queen discovers a portable public library on the grounds outside the royal kitchen. The bookmobile is there for the use of the palace staff. Ever polite, she borrows a book because she feels it would be rude otherwise. One book leads to another, and the Queen discovers the joys of reading for pleasure. Her literary guide is a minor palace character, Norman Seakins. (see Norman, p.24)

As the Queen reads more and more, and is involved in her duties less and less, her loyal servants and handlers are afraid, confused and even angered by how this newfound interested has thrown the monarchy and its activities into upheaval.

Keys to the Novel

The Uncommon Reader

- The phrase, "the uncommon reader", is adapted from Virginia Woolf's 1925 collection of essays called **The Common Reader**, a book that pays tribute to the act of reading for pleasure. But, Woolf, in turn, had reached back to Samuel Johnson who used the expression to honor all the ordinary readers for whom writers write.

- The word "common", defined by the dictionary as "ordinary", is actually anything but, and has several complex applications. First, it links together people who share things, places, and languages in common. Second, it describes the frequency of shared thoughts and activities, as in "commonly" held viewpoints. Third, it binds together the large mass of people who are less than royal in social and economic standing. These are the people in the mainstream of society: ordinary, work-classing folk, commoners who serve royalty. Situated directly opposite all of them is the Queen, who as head of the monarchy is, obviously, anything but common.

- The concept for Bennett's novel **The Uncommon Reader** came to him when he was returning home from a weekend in Yorkshire. He thought:

  > *What if the Queen began borrowing books from a mobile library and was transformed into a indefatigable reader? What if her family and her courtiers became first suspicious and then panicked by her new intellectual pursuit?* (Globe and Mail)

- It is in this sense that Alan Bennett plays with the concept of the uncommon reader – the definition, its significance, and its use to readers of all kinds. We watch with curiosity and delight as the Queen, who begins as a very common reader, grows to be a very astute and perceptive reader. (see The Power of Reading, p.29)

The Idea of Reading

- The theme of reading is the very large heart of this tiny book. It demonstrates how much Bennett treasures both the act of reading and its corollary, writing. He explores both through the perceptions and insights of the Queen as she changes from being a reader to becoming a writer.

- Reading functions in a variety of ways: instruction, information, provocation and pleasure. It is up to each individual to make a choice. Reading is an activity done informally for personal pleasure or as part of one's profession or job.

- Bennett uses the Queen's private and public persona to demonstrate that reading is both a self-contained and a collective process at the same time. While the Queen does not want to make reading a part of her public duties, she becomes increasingly eager to discuss books, authors and ideas with any interested person. (See Private, Public p.35)

- As he explores the idea of reading, Bennett reaches out to both common and uncommon readers with his unique and humorous writing style. (see Writing Style, p.43; Humor, Satire, p.44)

Author Information

- Alan Bennett was born on May 9, 1934 in the district of Armley in Leeds, Yorkshire. His father was a butcher and amateur musician and his mother, a homemaker. Bennett was hugely influenced by his father, whom he credits with giving him both a capacity for humor and a sense of self-deprecation. In truth, Bennett was once very shy, a situation overcome only through the use of laughter and comedy.

- Bennett attended Oxford University and graduated from there with a first-class degree in history. He planned to become a medieval historian, but stumbled into a career on the stage and screen.

- In 1960, Bennett and fellow Oxford students, Dudley Moore, Jonathan Miller and Peter Cook, appeared in **Beyond the Fringe** during the Edinburgh Festival. The show was a great success and continued performing in London and New York. This was the start of Bennett's fame.

- His first written stage play, **Forty Years On**, was produced in 1968. He has since written several dozen critically acclaimed plays. **The History Boys**, Bennett's most praised play to date, won three Olivier Awards in 2005, six Tony Awards in 2006, and went on to become a very successful film.

- His award-winning play **The Madness of George III** imagines the relationship between King George and Queen Charlotte after the king is diagnosed with lunacy (he suffered from an enzymatic disorder). It is based on Bennett's and his family's experiences with his mother's Alzheimer's illness. This play, too, went on to be a movie.

- Bennett has been offered several honorary degrees and has accepted many of them. But, guided by a unique sense of moral and ethical principles, he has refused others. For example, he rejected an honorary doctorate from Oxford to protest the university's act of naming a chair after media baron Rupert Murdoch, who was famously more interested in making money than in promoting honest journalism.

- In 1988, Bennett declined the King George Medal for excellence to the Empire, and he also refused a knighthood in 1996. He was concerned that by accepting these honors, he would take himself too seriously. In the case of the knighthood, it meant that he would have to meet the Queen in person and he preferred to let her dwell in the realm of his rich imagination. The only time Bennett has ever seen the Queen in person was in Leeds when he was a very young boy.
(Renzetti)

- Bennett is notoriously private and does not give many interviews. Therefore, most of his personal life, including his homosexuality, his fight with cancer, and his parents' struggles, remained a mystery until he published his memoirs, **Untold Stories**, in 2005. He began this personal story in 1997 after being diagnosed with cancer, because he believed his story would be published posthumously. He did not want to die only *"in the pages of a newspaper."* (BBC News)

- As he underwent treatment for his illness, his chance of survival was given to be less than fifty percent. Despite these long odds, Bennett found his bout with cancer to be unremarkable, writing that *"cancer, like any other illness, is a bore."* Thus far, he has survived and manages to keep himself, and us, entertained. (BBC News)

- Bennett currently lives in Camden Town in London, as he has for the past 31 years. His partner of 14 years is Rupert Thomas, a magazine editor thirty years his junior.

- Because Bennett's own life has included struggle, his usual characters are known for their unfortunate circumstances and downtrodden and meek demeanours. They represent the dramatic elements of his own life and personality and are often modeled after people Bennett knows or has met. (see Lady in the Van, p.50)

- Bennett is better known in Europe than in North America, so it is particularly delightful that his work has now crossed the ocean. In Britain, he is regarded as a national treasure. Due to his sharp, but warm and insightful humor, he also carries the tag of *"curmudgeon laureate."* (Edemariam) Bennett has had a very lengthy, successful and productive career and is considered one of the greatest living playwrights today. His thorough bibliography includes many award winning plays and other works. (see Bennett's Uncommon Works, p.56)

Background Information
Queen Elizabeth

- Queen Elizabeth II was born Elizabeth Alexandra Mary on April 21 1926, the first child born to Prince Albert, Duke of York, and Elizabeth, Duchess of York. She had one sibling, a younger sister, Princess Margaret, who was born in 1930 and who died in 2002.

- Growing up, it was never assumed that Elizabeth would become Queen, because her father had an older brother, Edward, Prince of Wales. When Elizabeth's grandfather, King George V, died in 1936, Edward succeeded the throne. However, he abdicated the position later that same year and Elizabeth's father was crowned King George VI, making Elizabeth the next in line.

- Queen Elizabeth II ascended the throne in 1952, upon her father's untimely death. She was twenty-six years old at the time.

- In 1947, Elizabeth married Prince Philip, Duke of Edinburgh. The couple had met several times as youngsters, but began a formal relationship in 1939, when Elizabeth was thirteen. Together, they have four children, Charles, Anne, Edward and Andrew and eight grandchildren.

- The British Commonwealth is made up of fifty-three independent states and territories. Among them are monarchies which include the United Kingdom, Canada, Australia, New Zealand, Jamaica, Barbados, the Bahamas, Grenada, Papua New Guinea, the Solomon Islands, Tuvalu, Saint Lucia, Saint Vincent and the Grenadines, Belize, Antigua and Barbuda, and Saint Kitts and Nevis, and others. These countries recognize the Queen as head of state, but in each region, she is represented by a Governor-General, who performs political and ceremonial functions on her behalf.

- Theoretically and historically, the Queen is very powerful (the Commonwealth has a population of nearly two billion people), but her role has become increasingly symbolic in nature and she rarely intervenes in politics.

- In 2002, the Queen celebrated her Golden Jubilee, the 50th year of her reign, but the celebrations were subdued because her mother and sister had died earlier in the year. The Jubilee festivities included an international tour of all her realms and a three day festival titled "Jubilee Days" which coincided with the Queen's 76th birthday. Despite predictions that the occasion would be a failure due to waning interest in the monarchy, the British people expressed a new-found interest and a respect for their long reigning queen.

- In 2006, Queen Elizabeth celebrated her 80th birthday. Although the Queen's real birthday is on April 21, it is customary that a crowned head celebrate their official birthday in June, to ensure better weather for the festivities. Celebrations included a children's party, church services and fireworks. The Queen also invited 99 people who were born on April 21, 1926 for a special birthday lunch.

- Queen Elizabeth has made it public that she has no intention to descend the throne any time soon. She is currently the third longest, and oldest, reigning monarch in British history. Prince Charles, her first-born son, is her designated successor.

Royal Hobbies

- Because the Queen is fiercely private, it is not known what kind of reader she is, if at all. In the National Year of Reading 1999, Westdale Junior School in Britain wrote to her asking about her favorite childhood books. Not wishing to play favorites, she politely declined to respond. **(Westdale Juniors)** But several members of the Royal family are avid supporters of the arts and culture.

- The Queen's established interests include horses, horse racing, photography and dogs. She actively breeds horses and dogs, and has even developed her own breed of dogs, the dorgi, when she crossed one of her corgi's with her sister's daschund.

- Prince Charles and Prince Philip are enthusiastic polo players. King George V was a stamp collector whose collection is considered one of the greatest in the world. Queen Victoria saved sketches and photographs.

- Famous regal writers include Henry VIII (the writer of political poetry and love songs), Queen Victoria (whose poetry and advice was not very "Victorian" in nature), and Elizabeth I (whose works include poetry, letters and speeches.)

- Bennett's Queen Elizabeth hopes to follow in the footsteps of both her namesake and Queen Victoria, although she does not intend to write like Victoria, as hers is *"a pretty tedious book ... so utterly without offense as to be almost unreadable. It is not a model one would want to follow."* (p.120, 121)

The Monarchy and the British Parliamentary System

- The Queen is the ceremonial head of the British Parliamentary system. The parliament is divided into three divisions: the upper house, the House of Lords; the lower house, the House of Commons; and the Queen. The House of Lords is not an elected body, its members are instead appointed by the queen upon recommendation by the Prime Minister. The House of Commons is democratically elected in elections which are held at least every five years.

- The prime minister, who is the leader of the party that holds the majority in the government, can come from either house, but usually he is a member of the House of Commons.

- In contemporary British politics, the prime minister has broad executive and legislative powers, but few statutory powers. He requires the support of the government in order to pass new legislation.

- In theory, the Queen is an essential part of the legislative process. She may, if she wishes, legally grant or withhold Royal Assent to Bills, but no monarch has done this since 1708. The Queen also reads the annual State Opening of Parliament speech, which outlines the government's legislative agenda for the coming year, a document that has been written by the ministers. However, the Queen does appoint the ministers, and all the government is carried out in her name.

- The Queen has a weekly meeting with the prime minister when parliament is in session. He updates her on the happenings in the government and solicits her advice on any number of matters. The Queen has access to all government documents and must sign all financial papers, executive orders and major transactions of state in order for them to be enacted.

The University of East Anglia

- The University of East Anglia, located in Norwich, England, is one of the top universities in the world with a reputation of developing and graduating internationally famous creative writers.

- Although Alan Bennett did not attend this school, some of its noted alumni are Ian McEwan, Kazuo Ishiguro, Anne Enright, Rose Tremain, Tracy Chevalier, and Trezza Azzopardi.

- And now, Norman Seakins can be added to the list.

CHARACTERIZATION

The Queen

Sir Kevin Scatchard

Norman Seakins

The Prime Minister

Sir Claude Pollington

CHARACTERIZATION

The Queen

- The Queen, as Alan Bennett imagines her in **The Uncommon Reader,** is a fictionalized character. Bennett uses the known aspects of her public persona to conceptualize her private personality. He doesn't stray too far from how she is traditionally portrayed, he just makes her warmer.

- We are introduced to a queen who is keenly loyal to her royal duties. Her sense of obligation is insurmountable; she is very much the "perfect" monarch, making the appropriate small talk when necessary and attending public functions and forums. But because she is so dedicated to her role, she has not had the time to develop her own interests. That is until, by chance, she discovers books in the palace's traveling library.

- When the Queen meets Norman and Mr. Hutchings, she is politely hesitant when they offer her the loan of a library book, because she doesn't know what to choose.

  She'd never taken much interest in reading. She read, of course, as one did, but liking books was something she left to other people. It was a hobby and it was in the nature of her job that she didn't have hobbies. (p.6)

- Bennett portrays hobbies as having no proper place in the palace because hobbies create preferences and preferences create division. In order to be a true Queen, equitable to everyone, she feels obliged to be neutral in order to maintain an air of inclusivity.

  Her job was to take an interest, not to be interested herself. (p.7)

- At first, the Queen is largely indiscriminatory in her reading and quickly covers a wide range of writers and subjects, from Sylvia Plath to Lauren Bacall to Charles Dickens. She defers to Norman who directs her. As she gets into the rhythm of reading, she reads eagerly and often, embracing everything from popular British literature to the classics.

  That the Queen could readily switch from showbiz autobiography to the last days of a suicidal poet seem both incongruous and wanting in perception. But, certainly in her early days, to her all books were the same and, as with her subjects, she felt a duty to approach them without prejudice. (p.49, 50)

- Soon, reading causes her to reconsider things about herself that she has always taken for granted, including the question of the monarchy and her role within it. This depth of insight threatens to cause problems. (see Monarchy, p.36)

> *It was reading, and love it though she did, there were times when she wished she had never opened a book and entered into other lives. It had spoiled her. Or spoiled her for this, anyway.* (p.62, 63)

- Reading helps her see and understand the world from a variety of different perspectives and this connects the Queen to her subjects in a new philosophical way.

   > *The appeal of reading, she thought, lay in its indifference: there was something lofty about literature. Books did not care who was reading them or whether one read them or not. All readers were equal, herself included. Literature, she thought, is a commonwealth; letters a republic.* (p.31)

- However, in reality, her amateur interest in books throws the royal routine into disarray, as she discovers she'd much rather spend time reading than performing her royal responsibilities. Her relish for discussing her stories causes events to run too long and creates some tension when she interacts with her followers. They expect impersonal topics, such as the traffic or the weather. No one is quite prepared to talk about their favorite books.

   > *It transpired that with no prior notification to her attendants the Queen had abandoned her long-standing lines of inquiry – length of service, distance travelled, place of origin – and had embarked on a new conversational gambit, namely, 'What are you reading at the moment?' To this very few of Her Majesty's loyal subjects had a ready answer (though one did try: 'The Bible?' ... Unsurprisingly the audiences got longer and more ragged, with a growing number of her loving subjects going away regretting that they had not performed well ...* (p.42)

- The Queen is a very driven woman, an attribute that defines her reign. She tries to constantly surpass herself, and one can see this self-competitiveness as the Queen becomes a better and better reader. At first, she reads out of obligation, then for pleasure, followed by insight. Eventually she engages more interactively with her books by making interpretive notes.

- At the end of the book, when it seems that neither she nor her reading can progress any further, she gives up the throne and considers becoming a writer. (Actually, with her new skills, the Queen could also become a terrific book club leader and presenter.)

- She feels, and rightly so, that with her experience and perspective she could write something that could *"transcend circumstances and stand on its own, a tangential history of its times ... far from ... politics or the events of one's life."* (p.122) Like Emily Dickinson, the Queen would like *"to tell the truth but tell it slant,"* (p.122) that is from her own unique frame of reference. She is, after all, not a common reader or thinker. She has been born and bred as a monarch.

The fictional prime minister nervously, but incorrectly, anticipates that the Queen would write a "tell-all" book. Consider what you would like to read in a book written by the Queen.

Sir Kevin Scatchard

- Sir Kevin Scatchard is the Queen's personal secretary. As a native of New Zealand and a graduate of Harvard Business School, Sir Kevin is considered an odd choice for the role of personal secretary, but his demeanor is highly professional and loyal. His selection represents a more modern and inclusive side of the Crown.

    Sir Kevin had been inevitably hailed in the press as a new broom, a young(ish) man who would sweep some

> *of the redundant deference and more flagrant flummeries that were monarchy's customary accretions, the Crown in this version as not unlike Miss Havisham's wedding feast - the cob-webbed chandeliers, the mice-infested cake and Sir Kevin as Mr Pip tearing down the rotting curtains to let in the light.* (p.27)

- Actually, Sir Kevin is a pompous and precise fellow who appears to have no personal life whatsoever outside of his job and the Queen. One of his major goals is to make the monarchy more accessible. Therefore, he is frustrated by the Queen's new pastime because it impacts on her day-to-day routines and alters the public's perception of her.

- Although he doesn't like her reading, Sir Kevin tries to turn it to his advantage by using it as a public relations stepping stone. When the Queen refuses to play along, he goes so far as to "lose" a case of books that she packed to take with her on a trip to Calgary and, while she is away, he disposes of Norman.

- Fed up with Sir Kevin's antics, the Queen retaliates by offering him a place as a high commissioner in New Zealand. Kevin sees this as the ultimate snub, but he should be happy. In times gone by, he would have not only lost his place in the palace, but his title and his head as well.

- Of the Commonwealth countries, New Zealand is one that separates the monarchy from the government. The country has held lively debates on the role of the monarchy and has had some issues with the use of royal titles. But times are changing, and they are planning to restore the use of monikers like "Sir" and "Dame". Sir Kevin will be safe on his return.

Norman Seakins

- Norman comes by his name honestly. Although it has Germanic roots, it is a popular English name and means *man from the north*. Alan Bennett would relate most closely to Norman's character because he too hails from the north of England.

- Norman is a simple kitchen aide, who is also a patron of the palace's traveling library. When Norman meets the Queen in the library trailer, they forge a relationship of sorts over books. Norman, who is an avid reader, becomes the Queen's docent to reading and literature.

- Norman is mild and relatively unassuming. Being very "book" smart, he appears to be a bit nerdy and to lack social confidence. In reality, however, Norman is quite at ease with himself, especially in his role as reading coach to the Queen. Norman is one of the Queen's few servants who is able to engage her in a "normal" conversation, without deferring to her royal stature or the established hierarchy in the palace. *"Oddity though he was, Norman was himself and seemed incapable of being anything else. This was very rare."* (p.17)

- The plot thickens when Sir Kevin becomes fed up with Norman's influence over the Queen. As punishment, he arranges to send Norman to the University of East Anglia. This sentencing backfires because it gives Norman access to an excellent education he could not otherwise have achieved on his own, and, ironically, it is Sir Kevin who is firmly and permanently sacked when the Queen uncovers the ruse.

How do each of these characters influence the Queen's reading habits? Would she have become such an avid reader without Norman's support or, likewise, without Sir Kevin's disapproval?

The Prime Minister

- The Queen's prime minister is never named and remains an ambiguous and faceless character throughout the book. With the modern timeset of the novel and, given Alan Bennett's political outlook, it is highly likely that this character is symbolic of, or at least similar to, Tony Blair, the prime minister of Great Britain at the time of 9/11.

- In Bennett's novel, the fictional prime minister represents the country's divided opinion on the relevance of the monarchy. Mr. Blair considered the Queen and other members of the royal family to be out of touch with the country. Likewise, Bennett's prime minister also sees the monarchy as archaically holding Britain back from her true potential as a democratic country. Just as the real Queen had no animosity towards Mr. Blair, the fictional Queen tolerates this upstart prime minister, in the same way he does her. (see Monarchy, p.36)

- The prime minister is one of the many subjects and servants who does not like nor understand the Queen's new interest in reading.

    [She] felt not unlike an air hostess going through the safety procedures, [while] the look on the prime minister's face [was] that of benevolent and minimal attention from a passenger who has heard it all before. (p.87)

- However, this does not mirror Bennett's feeling about the Queen nor the monarchy. He enjoys the idea of having a "queen," but is content to keep her inside the boundaries of his own imagination. He has no wish for that picture to alter, as the Queen's does when she holds a party for her favorite writers.

    Authors ... were probably best met within the pages of their novels, and were as much creatures of the reader's imagination as the characters in their books. (p.54)

Sir Claude Pollington

- Sir Claude Pollington is an old friend and trusted advisor of the Queen. He entered royal service when he was eighteen, and when we meet him, he is ninety years old. He represents the longevity and integrity of tradition; he is the keeper of royal family secrets that have been around almost as long as the Queen herself.

   > *There was not much about the royal family to which Sir Claude had not been privy ... He had done duty in the many offices of the household, finally serving as private secretary to the Queen. Even when he had long retired his advice was frequently called on; he was a living embodiment of that establishment commendation 'a safe pair of hands'.* (p.91, 92)

- Sir Kevin turns to Sir Claude when he reaches his wits' end as to what to do about the Queen and her reading. He is convinced that Sir Claude is the only one the Queen will listen to and that, therefore, she will come to her senses and return to duty. For her part, she understands clearly that Sir Claude has been sent to sabotage her love for reading.

- Sir Claude means well, but he really has no idea what either Sir Kevin or the Queen are talking about. He falls asleep during both meetings. His visit, however, awakens in the Queen the understanding that she has no distinct inner voice that the people would recognize, whereas her outer voice offers an illusion of power, a rubber stamp for the opinions of the government. As the novel winds down, the Queen looks to remedy this situation.

FOCUS POINTS AND THEMES

The Power of Reading

The Reader

The Writer

Borrowing

Private Lives, Public Lives

The Monarchy

FOCUS POINTS AND THEMES

The Power of Reading

- Reading has many different powers which include the ability to entertain, to teach, to appreciate, to challenge, to impact and to change. At different points throughout the novel, the Queen uses reading for each of these purposes and more.

- When the Queen first gets involved in her reading, it moderately changes her routine. She likes it so much that when she feels ill one morning, she stays in bed with her book. *"'The Queen has a slight cold' was what the nation was told, but what it was not told, and what the Queen herself did not know, was that this was only the first of a series of accommodations, some of them far-reaching, that her reading was going to involve."* (p.15)

Is the Queen's action uncommon? Have you ever stayed away from work or an important engagement to do something for yourself? Why or why not?

- A positive thing the Queen notices about reading is that it makes her more observant. She begins to see things and people in a different light. For example, she might never before have noticed that Sir Kevin was a reading saboteur.

    > *Sir Kevin had a very muscular face, the Queen thought. He seemed to have muscles in his cheeks and when he frowned, they rippled. If she were a novelist, she thought, that might be worth writing down.* (p.39)

- Sir Kevin believes that reading is a selfish pastime that isolates the Queen from her subjects, but that if she is intent on pursuing it, perhaps she should *"harness [her] reading to some larger purpose – the literacy of the nation as a whole, for instance, the improvement of reading standards among the young ..."* (p.46)

- This is indeed a noble cause and gets the Queen thinking about the impact her reading makes on her immediate family and household. The staff finds her harder to manage, while her family is relieved to be left out of her intense gaze. However, her husband, the duke, is not so pleased with his imposed isolation. When he passes by, she would *"glance up briefly and raise a vague, acknowledging hand. 'Well, I'm glad somebody's happy,' said the duke as he shuffled off down the corridor."* (p.48)

Has reading had a specific impact in your life?

- One of the more difficult thoughts that the Queen encounters is that the sheer immensity of reading material in the world makes it impossible to ever catch up. Not only that, she laments all the things she has missed knowing, even with her very full and eventful life. But sad or not, the Queen cannot go back to her non-reading days.

- As she advances through author after author, her mind opens to all sorts of possibilities and new feelings. Reading prepares the Queen for new places, people, experiences, and, most opening of all, new perspectives, emotions and thoughts.

    > *What she was finding ... was how one book led to another, doors kept opening wherever she turned and the days weren't long enough for the reading she wanted to do.* (p.21)

    Consider and discuss if there is a single book, poem, or essay that has opened or challenged your imagination.

- Reading also has the gentle (or sometimes forceful) ability to dramatically alter a person's perspective by humanizing it. One of the Queen's most engaging and elegant thoughts about the power of reading is that *"You don't put your life into your books. You find it there."* (p.104)

    If you agree (or not) with this quote, use it as a springboard to discussion.

- The most essential truth about the power of reading is that it is one of life's greatest pleasures. Bennett brilliantly demonstrates this by using the Queen as his central character. As a head of state, she controls a great part of the real world. As a reader, she has the potential to own all of it.

    Discuss what the power of reading means to you.

The Reader

- Another of Bennett's rounded frames of reference is to look at all sides of being a passionate reader. Juxtaposing the Queen against the rest of us common readers is a strategic and excellent literary move. One of the early things the Queen is amazed to discover is that she is a human being, subject to life and fate, in the same way that the British and Commonwealth people are political subjects to her. With this layered image, Bennett demonstrates the commonality of all readers, regardless of rank, creed, or nationality.

- According to Bennett, dedicated novice readers have similar characteristics, making them easy to spot.

    o The newly enthusiastic reader sees life through the context of an author's plot, characters, and quotable phrases. As the Queen discovers, this can be annoying if done to excess.

    o The same is true of newly formed opinions and questions that come out of the books read. Of course, for the Queen, who is not permitted strong personal opinions and categorical answers, this is more dangerous than for the rest of us. Her prime minister speculates that her lack of inclusive and definitive thinking could lead people to *"think the world could not be managed. That way lay chaos. Or defeat at the polls, which was the same thing."* (p.59) Reading can lead one into deep and murky waters.

    o When a new reader embarks on a new book which can simply not be put down, everything suffers – personal appearance, punctuality, family, friends, work. It is possible to sacrifice everything for the pleasure of the next word.

What are some identifiable markers of older experienced readers? Can all readers be put onto the same page?

The Writer

- Writers play an important role in **The Uncommon Reader**. As the Queen becomes a more devoted reader, she seeks out writers to meet and to discuss their books. When she organizes an occasion for this lofty purpose, they either ignore her or make common small talk, something she is definitely not good at unless it is scripted. She resolves never again to meet writers in person, but to keep them safely behind the veil of her imagination. The Queen makes an exception for the excellent Canadian short story writer Alice Munro.

If you had the formal or informal opportunity to meet a living writer, would you do it? What would you choose to talk about? If you are a writer, what conversations would you like to have with your readers?

- Just as Bennett and other writers have done before her, the Queen progresses through familiar literary stages. She moves from reading multiple books, to noting and transcribing meaningful passages. Then, she begins to have her own critical thoughts, and finally, entertains the thought of becoming a writer herself.

- However, the transition from reading to writing is not necessarily a straight path. When the Queen meets with Sir Claude, he suggests that she become a writer, if only to *"get her off reading ... because in his experience writing seldom got done. It was a cul-de-sac. He had been writing his memoirs for twenty years and hadn't even written fifty pages."* (p.99)

- The Queen would certainly have much to write about. After all, she has met most of the interesting people in the world – politicians, heads of state, artists, musicians, novelists, poets, businessmen and women, ordinary and extraordinary people. Her special experiences as a monarch would shape and inform her unique perspective.

- One of the Queen's moving realizations is her awareness that when she dies, she would exist in people's memories only as a statistical entry in a history book. Becoming a writer could change that because, while reading is listening to someone else's voice, writing is your own. The Queen is most interested in showcasing her own uncommon voice as the unique individual she is and *not*, as the prime minister and others worry, to write a tell-all book.

Borrowing

- In a beautiful play on words, the idea of "borrowing," is a key theme in the novel. It begins when the Queen borrows her first library book. Despite the fact that the palace has its own special library, it is not a place in which she feels comfortable reading a book. So she casually sends Norman to fetch books from the London Library, famously established in 1841 with the help of Thomas Carlyle, a Scottish satirical writer and historian. Norman is amazed at being able to borrow books from this exceptional collection.

- As her eagerness for reading grows, Norman brings her books from other public libraries. Then, one day, the Queen, who is usually well-informed, learns that the travelling library has been taken off her route due to financial cutbacks. Here Bennett introduces a small political jab at the whimsical nature of some current fiscal practices.

  > *Mr Hutchings told him that though he had pointed out to the Libraries Outreach Department that Her Majesty was one of their borrowers this cut no ice with the council, which, prior to axing the visits, said that inquiries had been made at the palace and it had disclaimed any interest in the matter.* (p.26)

  Of course, the question was never put to the Queen herself.

- Bennett is not content to leave the matter at this superficial level. Using countless literary and artistic references, he touches on the boundaries of literary "borrowing" beyond the use of a library lending card.

- Bennett grants that all artists, including writers, borrow from each other and, in this way, build a better art form. A good example of this is Bennett's chosen title for this novel. (see this guide, Uncommon Reader, p.8) No thought is truly original because it stems from, is informed by, or is inspired by other thoughts. The Queen borrows ideas from the books she reads. At first she does not formulate her own thoughts, but transcribes passages that strike her fancy. Her subjects borrow suggestions of what their favorite next book will be from what the Queen is reading.

- This is not about plagiarism, but about literary progress and word architecture. Bennett himself is always eager to give credit to those he borrows from.

Private Lives, Public Lives

- Reading has two faces, public and private, just like the Queen and just like each of us. There is no more private act than reading. It is an intimate process between the book and the reader, but reading eventually changes the reader in a public way. The reader ends up thinking differently, feeling differently, and possibly acting differently than before.

- Throughout the story, the Queen wants to have some private time for herself, but finds that she is increasingly at odds with her public presence and must perform as her subjects know and expect. They do not want her to change because then they would have to revise their conventional responses to her. She cannot be public and private at the same time.

- While the Queen makes some effort to talk about her newfound passion with her subjects, they nervously try to reply in kind, offering up their favorite authors or books, most often the Bible, in an effort to impress her. Although the Queen means these conversations to be more interactive, they have the opposite effect, threatening to alter the public's understanding of the monarchy as an institution.

- By reading such writers as Jane Austen, the Queen learns more about the private and common variations of social issues including class structure, feminism, economic and gender issues. Having previously seen only her public's "public" face, reading opens the Queen up to their private mindset.

- Reading equalizes both her public and private spheres of life.

    Reading ... was anonymous; it was shared; it was common. And she who had led a life apart now found that she craved it. Here in these pages and between these covers she could go unrecognised." (p.32)

    But reading hasn't changed the essence of who the Queen is and what she does – it has just made her warmer and more flexible.

- A note of paradox is that Bennett is just as private as the Queen. He refuses many interviews, and yet uses his work as a platform to analyze his very personal perspectives.

The Monarchy

- During Queen Elizabeth's fifty year reign, there have been many social, economic, political and cultural changes. Yet, the Queen has remained steadfast in carrying out her royal roles and responsibilities. Although biographers, journalists, artists and dramatists have attempted to capture the essence of the Queen's private nature, she remains an enigma to the world.

- Because he's never met the Queen, Alan Bennett doesn't claim to interpret her. His goal is simply to imagine her by using real facts, valid comparisons, and true psychological insight. As a result, Bennett figuratively disrobes the Queen and allows her to dress more commonly. He speculates that underneath the pomp and ceremony, she might actually wish, at times, to be a common person.

- The direction of this thought leads to a look at the monarchy – what it represents, its importance, and its ability to endure. Bennett is not critical of the monarchy nor does he advocate its end, but gently suggests that it could benefit from some literary redemption. After all, the Queen doesn't live in an isolated political republic, removed from her subjects. In this novel, she lives in a virtual "republic of letters," one that unites all its citizens under the universal banner of common humanity.

- Bennett admires the royals and feels *"they really do work their arses off in a way which goes well beyond even being conscientious."* (Dudding)

- Reading becomes everyone's redemption. If the monarchy can regain a sense of relevancy through the Queen's act of reading, then her subjects might discover a better socialized, enlightened leader. (see Uncommon Readers, p.51)

- Bennett uses the Queen to poke gentle fun at the rigid bureaucracy of government. He wants both bureaucrats and royals to acknowledge the presence of the people who prop them up on their respective pedestals. He does the same thing with all the long-winded and self-indulgent writers that he references in the novel. The lesson presented is that it is not possible to have a monarchy, society, or readership without substantial common support.

- The role of the monarchy, and the public's expectations of it have changed over time, and again Bennett quietly prompts readers to remember that the monarchy is the solid baseline which defines Britain. This novel is not a call to change; change will come regardless. Bennett subtly argues not to forget or forego the past, but to build on it.

- A lesser writer might have used the opportunity to launch an extensive public discussion about the continued existence of the monarchy. Bennett acknowledges the debate but folds into it the country's deep love for the Queen. It is this love that pushes readers to want to know her more intimately.

- There is a delightful historic parallel. Queen Elizabeth II was crowned in 1952, the result of her uncle's decision to abdicate the throne in order to live a different life by marrying the woman he loved. In **The Uncommon Reader,** the Queen hints that she is prepared to leave the throne in order to become a writer and thus take her life in a new direction to pursue something she is growing to love.

- The real Queen Elizabeth, however, has made it clear she has no intention of stepping down anytime soon. That being said, the Queen is over eighty years old and cannot live forever.

What are your thoughts about the British monarchy? Is your perspective contingent on where you live – eg., Britain, the United States, in a Commonwealth country? Will the concept of monarchy continue to have a role in our changing global society?

WRITING STYLE AND STRUCTURE

The Novel's Framework

Writing Style

Humor and Satire

WRITING STYLE AND STRUCTURE

If we could reduce this novel like a sauce, by boiling out its extraneous thoughts and details, we would end up with an essence that is both sweet and savory. This elixir asks questions about why we read and write. The answer is simple, yet complex, and impossible to categorize in black and white terms. Bennett has cooked up a blend of perspectives and lays them all out before us in the sparest of narratives.

The Novel's Framework

- The novel takes place towards the end of the Queen's life. The short timespan of the story bookmarks the last few years of her reign and ends with her Golden Jubilee celebrations of 2002.

- The book's structure is loose. The Queen is just the vehicle to fill in the spaces between Bennett's theories. We don't know much about the Queen personally, in the same way that we don't know everything about the intricate organization of the monarchy. Bennett fills the gaps with warmth and humor. His caricatures do not demean royalty, but augment its humaneness and raise it up to a higher level. At the same time, he hoists the concept of reading onto a similar plane.

- **The Uncommon Reader** counts only 121 pages. While this length allows us to explore a tiny part of the Queen's long and rich life, it doesn't miss much in terms of her developing outlook, and it proves that one is never too old to think new thoughts.

- Physically, this very elegant book would fit well into a regally gloved hand. It is a book fit for a queen. In the hardcover edition of this novel, the paper has a lovely rich feel and, inside the covers, there are graceful floral decorations laid out in gold and royal blue. The typeset is delicate and sophisticated. The cover picture on the Faber and Faber published edition has a pair of gold reading glasses positioned under the title, which is capped by the royal crown.

- The crown is slightly askew, suggesting that the Queen is so highly engrossed in her reading that she forgets to maintain her public stance. Another way of looking at the tipped crown is that it can proclaim each common reader as uncommon. To paraphrase Tolstoy, every reader is distinct in his or her own way. With this novel, Bennett, and not the Queen, bestows rank upon everyone.

- The book leaves us with an ambiguous ending. Although, the Queen insinuates that she is planning to abdicate the throne to become a writer, in real life she is still the Queen.

How did you feel about the shortness of the book and its ending? Is there anything you wished Bennett had explored more fully?

Writing Style

- Alan Bennett can be described as a warm and genial writer. He is not aloof, yet his writing is formal and follows tradition when discussing the monarchy. He gives all characters their proper titles even when discussing them in the third person. Secondary characters are introduced by their full or proper names, for example, the author "Ms Munro."

- Bennett's dignified narration respects the distance between the Queen and the rest of us. He is very fond of both her and her position, and although he follows the tradition of formality, he builds into it a sense of intimacy. He portrays the Queen in a different light, using his story to bridge the spaces between the reader and the monarch and to reinforce the positive attributes of this solemn and long-standing system of leadership.

- The narrative style of the novel feels like a monologue despite the many ongoing conversations. Monologues are traditionally one-sided perspectives told by the characters in a play and Bennett is first and foremost a playwright.

- It is clear, though, that Bennett's voice is an original one. There is only one Alan Bennett, just as there is only one Queen Elizabeth II.

Consider Bennett's writing techniques. How are they effective?

Humor and Satire

- One of Alan Bennett's strongest assets as a writer is his powerful, dry wit and **The Uncommon Reader** no exception. Bennett has always been a very funny man who uses humor as therapy and as a vehicle to offer up his unique take on the world. His critics refer to it as a *"Bennettian view ... that is every bit as identifiable and as singular as a Pinteresque one."* (The reference is to Harold Pinter.)

    To him, nothing and nobody are quite what they seem. Normalness is an aberration. For every dark side there is a sort of humorous underside. It's seeing the paradoxical nature of things that's his identifying mark – and a sort of optimistic gloom. (Lyall)

- Bennett creates humor by playing one subject against another. For example, with the evident contrast between the book **My Dog Tulip** and the Queen's own passion for dogs, Bennett gently satirizes the world of gays and lesbians.

- Bennett's Queen struggles with her own sense of social comedy. Until she started reading for insight, she never understood the charms of writer Jane Austen. Initially, she chose not to read Austen, simply because every one had already tried to persuade her. But once she opens an Austen novel, she sees they are right. In addition, when she gets into the rhythm of reading, she allows herself to be critical of writers like Henry James and Samuel Johnson who seem long-winded.

    'Am I alone', she wrote, 'in wanting to give Henry James a good talking-to?'
    "I can see why Dr Johnson is well thought of, but surely, much of it is opinionated rubbish?" (p.51)

- Next Bennett takes all of the Queen's real characteristics and exaggerates them slightly, until they become very funny. For example, the Queen is well-known for her famous small-handed wave from the back seat of her car.

  > *She'd got quite good at reading and waving, the trick being to keep the book below the level of the window and to keep focused on it and not on the crowds. The duke didn't like it one bit, of course, but goodness it helped.* (p.33)

- The common nature of her feelings, including those of boredom, endear her and bring her closer to us. Humor enlarges the Queen's emotions and shrinks the gap between hers and ours.

- There is also a sweet irony in the fact that Bennett will earn "royalties" from his introspective discussion about the royalty that is the subject of these delightful pages.

LAST THOUGHTS

Fictionalizing the Queen

The Lady in the Van

Uncommon Readers

Bennett's Uncommon Works

The Queen's Reading List

Suggested Beginnings

LAST THOUGHTS

Fictionalizing the Queen

- Recently, several major works of art have fictionalized the Queen's life while she is still in power. A notable and recent portrayal is the 2006 film, **The Queen,** which stars Helen Mirren and examines, in part, the repercussions of Princess Diana's death on the Queen and her government. The film's director, Steven Frears, is a good friend and frequent collaborator of Alan Bennett.

- A different, but equivalent example, is the 2008 Oliver Stone film, **W,** which explored the life and presidency of George W. Bush. This film was released while Bush was still the American president.

- Emotionally intimate portrayals such as these have the ability to influence the public's perception of these very public figures.

- Bennett has depicted royalty before, for example, in his play **The Madness of King George**. Bennett does not pick sides (royal vs. non-royal), instead he humanizes what appears to be a rigid institution. He deflates the superficial impression of pomposity and allows everyone to be approachable. In a note of interest, Helen Mirren played the role of Queen Catherine in the 2002 film version of **The Madness of King George**. Clearly, she has the touch of royalty about her.

- Bennett has also fictionally represented the Queen in a 1991 TV play, **A Question of Attribution**. At the time, Queen Elizabeth was asked for her reaction to her film persona. She quipped, *"she makes wisecracks. You see I don't make wisecracks."* (Dudding) And yet, Elizabeth has been photographed, often and beautifully, showing off her majestic smile and twinkling eyes. Bennett clearly sees a different person behind the mask.

Is an artistic fictional portrayal appropriate while its subject is actively in office? Has your opinion about any particular public figure been affected by such a presentation? How and why?

The Lady in the Van

- Here is a small story to illustrate the complexity and humanity of Alan Bennett. One day in 1974, Bennett saw that a van was parked down the street from his home for some length of time. The lady living in the van was Mary Shepherd. She was old and eccentric.

- Bennett invited her to park the van in his driveway, stipulating that it would be for three months, and after that she would then have to find another suitable location. The three months lasted fifteen years until her death. He wrote a play about it called **The Lady in the Van**. It opened at the Queen's Theatre in London in 1999, starring Maggie Smith.

- Perhaps the lady lives on in the traveling library parked in the Queen's driveway.

Uncommon Readers

- The notion of an uncommon reader is different than that of a reluctant reader. The Queen never struggled with literacy, but rather had never considered that having a dedicated interest in literature could be important. She had other vital interests competing for her attention, such as worldly events and affairs.

- Many people today face the same time constraints in their jobs and daily lives. Also vying for everyone's attention is the diversity of modern entertainment sources. There is no longer a common denominator that attracts or defines a single audience. For many people, reading is an activity that easily falls off the radar screen and so Bennett raises the issue and brings it to the forefront.

- Part of Bennett's delightful presentation of the Queen as an uncommon reader is the prominence of her role in society. As a public figure with public roles and responsibilities, she is juxtaposed with the very private activity of reading. (See Private, Public, p.35)

- People expect different things from today's leaders than they once did. To be sure, there is no alternative to successful economic and fair-minded administration, but present-day citizens also look for an emotional tie. Bennett's Queen comes to understand that she can improve her connection to her citizens through an expanded sense of literacy. A parallel inference is that other heads of state should also be able to do the same.

- Literature often portrays and shapes the public's perception of many prominent figures, including celebrities, presidents and prime ministers. Therefore, the idea of a leadership enlightened by reading leads to a look at other world leaders and their individual philosophies of governance. A survey of some relevant and noteworthy leaders in this section may make interesting reading.

Consider what you expect or want from your elected leaders. How would a leader's specific approach to reading affect your vote?

Barack Obama

- On January 20, 2009, Barack Obama was inaugurated as the 44th president of the United States. President Obama is a very avid reader. In speeches and interviews, he often mentions the books he is reading or is influenced by. He cites William Shakespeare, Ralph Waldo Emerson, Toni Morrison, and Ernest Hemingway among his favorite authors. He especially likes Morrison's **Song of Solomon**, Hemingway's **For Whom the Bell Tolls**, and Herman Melville's **Moby Dick**.

  > *"I had tons of books,"* Obama says in his biography. *"I read everything. I think that was the period when I grew as much as I had ever grown intellectually. But it was a very internal growth."* (Salon)

- Obama's literary references are so prominent and frequent that they cause the sales of the books he references to skyrocket. The online bookstore AbeBooks has compiled a complete list of Obama's favorite books, drawn from his interviews, speeches, photographs and more. (www.abebooks.com/books/barack-obama)

- The president has also written two memoirs: **Dreams From My Father**, about his atypical and multiracial upbringing and **The Audacity of Hope**, which outlines his political ideologies and his first term in the US Senate.

How do you feel about a literary president? If you have read Obama's books, did they change your ideas about him and his persona as a public figure? If not, why not?

George Bush

- Throughout Bush's presidency, there was a circulating joke that his favorite book was Eric Carle's classic children's story, **The Very Hungry Caterpillar**. The quip stemmed from an interview in which Bush claimed that as a child, this was his best-liked book. However, it wasn't published until 1969, when Bush was 23 years old. To be fair, perhaps he meant that he read it to his daughters.

- In 2008, Karl Rove, the deputy chief-of-staff at the time, published an article in the Wall Street Journal that outlined Bush's literary inclinations. According to Rove, he and the president began a reading competition to see who could read the most titles. This started as a New Year's Resolution and became a contest in the years 2006 to 2008. In the first year, Bush lost to Rove: 95 books to 110. In 2007 and 2008, the total number of books Bush read were considerably reduced.

- George Bush finds reading relaxing and pleasant. He prefers to read biographies of such people as Abraham Lincoln, Mark Twain, Babe Ruth, William Jennings Bryan, King Leopold, Lyndon B. Johnson and Genghis Khan. The one constant entry on Bush's reading list is the Bible which he reads in its entirety each year.

- Laura Bush, the president's wife, is a former librarian. A very active reader, she campaigned for literacy throughout her terms as First Lady of the United States.

Do you consider George Bush a literary person? If so, why has this been downplayed throughout his presidency? Compare and contrast Bush's public face with that of his successor, Barack Obama.

Tony Blair

- To continue the discussion on public and private perspectives, we can look at the past and current British prime ministers, Tony Blair and Gordon Brown. On the surface, Blair possesses much outward charm as opposed to the quieter Gordon Brown.

- According to the timeline of **The Uncommon Reader,** it is likely that Bennett's portrayal of the unnamed prime minister is based on Tony Blair, Britain's prime minister from May 1997 to June 2007.

- Blair's penchant for books is pale compared to his successor, Gordon Brown. Blair claims **Ivanhoe** by Sir Walter Scott to be his favorite book and cites Leo Tolstoy, Robert Louis Stevenson and J. R. R. Tolkien as three of his preferred authors. (Times)

- Blair rarely talks about the books he is currently reading or has read in the past. In a now famous public meeting, Blair mistook the very well-known Ian McEwan for an artist instead of the iconic author that he is.

- Blair claims that he does not have time to read, and that when he does, they are usually children's books. He has four young children.

Does knowing the literary interests and habits of our political leaders affect your opinion of them? Why or why not? How important is a warm and friendly public face on a public figure? What if the face masks a completely different personality underneath?

Gordon Brown

- The current prime minister of Britain is the Scottish-born Gordon Brown, who succeeded Tony Blair on June 27, 2007 after Blair resigned. Before being named prime minister, Brown served as Chancellor of the Exchequer in Blair's Labour government.

- Gordon Brown is a stark contrast to the fictional prime minister in **The Uncommon Reader.** He loves books and reading, and talks often about both. He makes a point of keeping up to date with the most popular non-fiction books and actively discusses his literary likes and dislikes with his aides, cabinet members and other elected officials. Like Bennett's Queen, Brown will ask the people he meets *"What are you reading?"* instead of the usual *"How are you doing?"*

    "I was brought up in a house where books were not just in one room but in every room," Brown said in an interview. *"My father seemed to have bought the whole book collection of Scotland."* (Prospect)

- **Prospect Magazine** calls Gordon Brown *"one of the best read politicians of our time."* Brown often cites authors and books in his speeches and lists such greats as George Orwell, Matthew Arnold, Winston Churchill, Tolstoy, Wordsworth, Tennyson, Thomas Gray, H. G. Wells, and Milton among his favorite authors.

Stephen Harper

- Because Bookclub-in-a-Box is a Canadian enterprise, it is only fair to also consider **Stephen Harper,** Canada's current prime minister, as a member of the "uncommon readers" section, especially because, on the surface, Harper also appears to be less literary than his rival political figures. For example, Michael Ignatieff, the present leader of the opposition, has written sixteen books, both fiction and non-fiction, and has taught at both Harvard and Oxford Universities.

- Under Harper, federal support for literacy and the arts has faltered. His relationship with the press and with the artistic community is less than positive. In the latest 2008 Canadian federal election, Harper so enraged the famous author Margaret Atwood, that she spearheaded a political movement called **"Anyone but Harper."**

- Canadian writer Yann Martel, famous for his book **Life of Pi**, has also taken Stephen Harper's literary education to heart. Every two weeks since April 2007, Martel has sent Stephen Harper a book he thinks the prime minister should read. Martel believes that there are lessons in books that can be applied to the political challenges that any government official faces. You can see the complete list and a copy of Martel's original letters on the website www.whatisstephenharperreading.ca.

- Stephen Harper has never spoken publicly about this project, and has responded to Martel only once in a thank you response, written by his personal secretary, for the book **The Death of Ivan Ilych**.

What do you think of Yann Martel's project? What books would you ask your political leaders to read? Why?

Bennett's Uncommon Works (Bibliography)

Books:

Beyond the Fringe (with Peter Cook, Jonathan Miller, and Dudley Moore) (1963)
Forty Years On (1969)
Getting On (1972)
Habeas Corpus (1973)
The Old Country (1978)
Enjoy (1980)
Office Suite (1981)
Objects of Affection (1982)
A Private Function (1984)
The Writer in Disguise (1985)
Prick Up Your Ears: The Film Screenplay (1987)
Two Kafka Plays (1987)

Talking Heads (1988)
Single Spies (1989)
The Lady in the Van (1989)
Poetry in Motion (with others) (1990)
The Wind in the Willows (1991)
The Madness of George III (1992)
Poetry in Motion 2 (with others) (1992)
Writing Home (memoir & essays) (1994)
The Laying on of Hands (novella) (2000)
The Clothes They Stood Up In (novella) (2001)
Untold Stories (autobiographical and essays) (2005)
The Uncommon Reader (novella) (2007)

Television:

My Father Knew Lloyd George (also writer) (1965)
Famous Gossips (1965)
Plato—The Drinking Party (1965)
Alice in Wonderland (1966)
On the Margin series (actor & writer) (1966-67)
A Day Out (also writer) (1972)
Sunset Across the Bay (also writer) (1975)
A Little Outing (also writer) (1975)
A Visit from Miss Prothero (writer) (1978)
Me—I'm Afraid of Virginia Woolf (writer) (1978)
Doris and Doreen (Green Forms) (writer) (1978)
The Old Crowd (writer) (1979)
Afternoon Off (actor & writer) (1979)
One Fine Day (writer) (1979)
All Day On the Sands (writer) (1979)
Objects of Affection (also writer) (1982)
The Merry Wives of Windsor (actor) (1982)
An Englishman Abroad (writer) (1983)

The Insurance Man (writer) (1986)
Breaking Up (1986)
Man and Music (narrator) (1986)
Talking Heads (also writer) (1987)
Down Cemetery Road (presenter) (1987)
Fortunes of War series (actor) (1987)
Dinner at Noon (narrator) (1988)
102 Boulevard Haussmann (writer) (1990)
A Question of Attribution (writer) (1991)
Selling Hitler (1991)
A Dance to the Music of Time (actor) (1997)
Talking Heads 2 (1998)

Films:

Long Shot (1980)
Dreamchild (voice only) (1985)
The Secret Policeman's Ball (1979)
The Secret Policeman's Other Ball (1982)
A Private Function (screenplay) (1986)
Pleasure At Her Majesty's (1987)
Prick Up Your Ears (screenplay) (1987)
Little Dorrit (1987)
Wind in the Willows animated adaptation (1994)
Parson's Pleasure (writer) (1995)
The Madness of King George (screenplay, adapted)(1995)
The History Boys (screenplay, adapted) (2006)

Radio

The Great Jowett (1980)
Dragon (1982)
Uncle Clarence (writer, narrator) (1985)

Better Halves (narrator) (1988)
The Lady in the Van (writer, narrator) (1990)
Winnie-the-Pooh (narrator) (1990)

Stage

Better Late (1959)
Beyond the Fringe (also co-writer) (1960)
The Blood of the Bambergs (1962)
A Cuckoo in the Nest (1964)
Forty Years On (also writer) (1968)
Sing a Rude Song (co-writer) (1969)
Getting On (writer) (1971)
Habeas Corpus (also writer) (1973)
The Old Country (writer) (1977)
Enjoy (writer) (1980)
Kafka's Dick (writer) (1986)
A Visit from Miss Prothero (writer) (1987)
Single Spies (1988)
The Wind in the Willows (adaptation) (1990)
The Madness of George III (writer) (1991)
Talking Heads (also writer) (1992)
The History Boys (writer) (2004)

Prizes and Awards:

1961   Evening Standard Award for Best Play   Beyond The Fringe
1962   New York Drama Critics Award (Special Citation) Beyond The Fringe
1963   Tony Special Award   Beyond The Fringe
1967   BAFTA Comedy Award   On The Margin TV series
1968   Evening Standard Award   Forty Years On
1971   Evening Standard Award   Getting On

1977 Critics' Circle Award   The Old Country
1984 Broadcasting Press Guild Award   An Englishman Abroad
1984 Royal Television Society Award   An Englishman Abroad
1985 BAFTA (Best Film Award)   A Private Function
1985 BAFTA (Best Original Screenplay) (nomination)
A Private Function
1986 LCCFA Best Screenwriter of the Year Award
A Private Function
1986 Royal Television Society Award   The Insurance Man
1988 BAFTA (Best Adapted Screenplay) (nomination)
Prick Up Your Ears
1988 LCCCFA Best Screenwriter of the Year Award
Prick Up Your Ears
1989 Hawthornden Prize   Talking Heads
1990 Laurence Olivier Award for Best Comedy   Single Spies
1991 BAFTA (Best Single Drama)   A Question of Attribution
1995 Academy Award for Best Adapted Screenplay (nomination)
The Madness of King George
1995 Writers' Guild Award (Best Adapted Screenplay)
The Madness of King George
1996 BAFTA (Best Adapted Screenplay) (nomination)
The Madness of King George
1996 LCCFA Best Screenwriter of the Year
The Madness of King George
1999 BAFTA (Best Single Drama) (nomination)   Talking Heads 2
2000 Laurence Olivier Award for Best New Play (shortlist)
The Lady In The Van
2003 British Book Awards Lifetime Achievement Award
2004 Critics' Circle Award for Best New Play   The History Boys
2004 Evening Standard Award for Best Play of the Year
The History Boys
2004 Whatsonstage.com Award for Best New Comedy
The History Boys
2005 Laurence Olivier Award for Best Play   The History Boys

2005   Society of London Theatres Special Award for Contribution to Theatre   The History Boys
2005   South Bank Show Award for Theatre   The History Boys
2006   British Book Awards Author of the Year   Untold Stories
2006   J. R. Ackerley Prize   Untold Stories
2006   New York Drama Critics' Award for Best Play   The History Boys
2006   New York Drama Desk Award for Outstanding New Play   The History Boys
2006   Samuel Johnson Prize (shortlist)   Untold Stories
2006   Tony Award for Best Play (US)   The History Boys
2006   Bollinger Everyman Wodehouse Prize (shortlist)   The Uncommon Reader
2008   Booksellers Association Independent Booksellers' Book Prize (shortlist)   The Uncommon Reader

The Queen's Reading List

- J.R. Ackerley (1896-1967) was a British magazine editor and writer. He was known for being open about his homosexuality at a time when it was very unpopular to do so. His 1956 novel **My Dog Tulip** was an account of his complicated relationship with his dog, Queenie (who was renamed Tulip for the novel), and how this relationship impacted his human connections. This book is included on the Queen's list for the obviously comedic link between the monarch and her dogs.

- Jane Austen (1775-1817) is one of the most widely read English novelists of all time. Her sharp observations and commentary on British class society are displayed in such classics as **Sense and Sensibility** (1811), **Pride and Prejudice** (1813), **Mansfield Park** (1814) and **Emma** (1815).

- Honoré de Balzac (1799-1850) was a French novelist and playwright. His one hundred novels and plays probe all facets of French life under the rule of Napoleon Bonaparte, and are collectively titled **La Comédie Humaine** *(The Human Comedy)*.

- Ivy Compton-Burnett (1884-1969) was an English novelist. She is best known for her novel **Mother and Son,** which was awarded the 1955 James Tait Black Memorial Prize.

- Joseph Conrad (1857-1954) was the Polish-born English writer of the 1899 novel **Heart of Darkness**. Although Conrad himself did not speak English until his twenties, he has greatly influenced English literature throughout the 20th century.

- Charles Dickens (1812-1870) is one of English literature's most popular British novelists, penning such classics as **Oliver Twist** (1837), **A Christmas Carol** (1843), **David Copperfield** (1850), **A Tale of Two Cities** (1859) and **Great Expectations** (1861).

- Emily Dickinson (1830-1886) is considered one of America's finest nature poets, but published only seven poems during her lifetime. The bulk of her nearly two thousand poems were brought out in their unedited form in 1955, seventy years after her death.

- Fyodor Dostoyevsky (1821-1881) was the Russian writer and philosopher who wrote **Crime and Punishment** (1866). Dostoyevsky exerted a significant influence on the existentialist movement.

- Henry Fielding (1707-1754), an English novelist and dramatist wrote the famous novel **Tom Jones** (1749) which is considered one of the first English novels ever published. Fielding was also one of the first novelists to openly admit that his works were purely fiction.

- E.M. Forster (1879-1970) was an English writer who wrote novels, short stories and essays. He is well known for his ironic and thoughtful novels that examined class difference and hypocrisy in Britain in the early 20th century. **Passage to India** is a literary classic.

- Jean Genet (1910-1986) was a French writer and political activist. Early in his life, he was a petty criminal. Turning to writing, he produced several poems, novels and plays that are well known today, including **The Thief's Journal, Our Lady of the Flowers, The Balcony, The Blacks** and **The Maids.**

- **Thomas Hardy** (1840-1928) fancied himself a poet and wrote novels to finance his poetry. Hardy was one of the leaders of the naturalist movement in literature - literature that seeks to replicate everyday life as opposed to literature that has more fantastical, romantic or surreal elements. His many classics include **The Mayor of Casterbridge** and **Tess of the D'Urbervilles.**

- **Christopher Isherwood** (1906-1986) is known for his stories about 1930s Berlin. His plays are based largely on his own life and often featured his literary friends, like Stephen Sender and Virginia Woolf, albeit under different names.

- **Henry James** (1843-1916) is known in literary circles as the master of the novel and novella form. Although he was born in the United States, he lived most of his life in England and eventually became a British citizen. His most serious contribution to literature was the idea of the internal monologue and the unreliable narrator, both of which prompt the Queen to tell him to *"get on"* with the story.

- **Nancy Mitford,** who lived from 1904-1973, was an English novelist and biographer. She was often called one of the "Bright Young Things" on the London social scene between the great wars. **The Pursuit of Love** was the first novel author Alan Bennett fell in love with, and is why he selected it as the first choice for the Queen. (Globe and Mail)

- **Alice Munro** (b. 1931) is a Canadian short-story author. Considered one of the greatest writers of the 20th century, and one of the greatest Canadian writers of all time, Munro's extensive works examine people's relationships in an effortless yet complex manner. Both Alan Bennett and his Queen admire Ms. Munro.

- **Sylvia Plath** (1932-1963) was an American novelist and poet. Her famous work **The Bell Jar** (1963) is a semi-autobiographical novel about a young girl who suffers a mental breakdown while working in New York. Plath is a great writer who committed suicide in 1963.

- **Anthony Powell** (1905-2000) was an English novelist, whose twelve volume book, **A Dance to the Music of Time,** was published between 1951-1975. He is compared to Marcel Proust for the similarity of their influence, unique writing style, irreverence and continuous popularity.

- **Marcel Proust** (1871-1922) was a French novelist and critic. He is best known for his seven-part work of fiction titled **In Search of Lost Time,** also published as **Remembrance of Things Past.** After the deaths of his parents, he openly practiced both homosexuality and bisexuality.

- **Mary Renault** (1905-1983), an English writer, is famous for her historical novels set in Ancient Greece and her biography of Alexander the Great. Her portrayals of Theseus, Socrates and Plato are well-known.

- **Philip Roth** (b. 1933) is an American novelist most famously known for his 1969 work **Portnoy's Complaint** as well as his prolific collection of novels based on the semi-autobiographical character, Nathan Zuckerman. Roth is an insightful commentator on the human condition.

- **Laurence Sterne** (1713-1768) was an Irish-born English novelist who penned the famous book, **The Life and Opinions of Tristram Shandy** (1759), a great comic novel.

- Ivan Turgenev (1818-1883), a Russian novelist and playwright, wrote the novel **Fathers and Sons** (1862).

- Denton Welch (1915-1948) was an English artist and writer. Born in Shanghai and raised in China, he wrote a fictionalized autobiography of his childhood in **Maiden Voyage** in 1935. His other well known works include **In Youth is Pleasure** (1943), **Brave and Cruel** (1949), and **A Voice through a Cloud** (1950, post-humously).

- Virginia Woolf (1882-1941), novelist and essayist, is considered one of the greatest literary figures of the 20th century. Her best known works include **Mrs Dalloway** (1925), **To the Lighthouse** (1927), **Orlando** (1928), **A Room of One's Own** (1929) and **The Common Reader** (1925). Woolf suffered from depression which greatly influenced her work; she took her own life in 1941.

What author or book would you recommend to the Queen and why?

Suggested Beginnings

1. The Queen becomes an avid reader late in life, reading indiscriminately and reading often. In reality, little is known about the Queen's reading preferences.

What do you imagine the Queen likes to read?

2. Most of the Queen's aides and servants were uncomfortable with her active reading habit.

Was the Queen's reading really so disruptive or are they simply uncomfortable with how this new interest reflects on them and their personal reading patterns?

3. The Queen must never play favorites and so, when she decides to give a dinner party for British writers, Sir Kevin is concerned that this will cause a rift among other artistic producers of culture.

Given the nature of celebrity today, could an active political interest in a particular author, sport or artist affect the public's reception of that person or pastime? Would this have a positive or negative effect?

4. When asked to select a book for the Queen, Norman chooses Ackerley's My Dog Tulip.

If given the same task, what book would you choose? Why?

5. At the end of the novel, the Queen feels she needs to take her reading to the next level, and become a writer herself.

What does this say about the Queen's character? Could all readers reach this point?

6. The Queen didn't consider reading as an activity until she visited the traveling library and had Norman help her with the book selection.

How important is Norman's role in developing the Queen's literary interests? Would she have become as avid a reader without him? How important is a literary role model to any reader?

7. The Queen is very dismissive of **Harry Potter**.

Given the Queen's humble readerly beginnings, why do you think she feels this way about one of Britain's, indeed the world's, most popular books?

8. Often, with the exception of Norman, the Queen's subjects do not engage in literary debate with her, but rather reaffirm the quality of the books she is reading.

Why are her subjects afraid to talk to her about books? What would your reaction be if a similar situation arose?

9. Bennett's fictionalization of the Queen is quite different from the movie starring Helen Mirren.

Compare and contrast the two representations of the Queen. Which do you prefer? Which do you think is more true-to-life?

10. **The Uncommon Reader** moves along at a quick and even pace. The reader has to keep up with the Queen in the same way that her staff and subjects do. Yet, she manages to catch them off-guard.

Did the ending surprise you? What were you expecting? How could Bennett have ended the novel more effectively?

FROM THE NOVEL

Quotes

FROM THE NOVEL ...

Memorable quotes from the text of The Uncommon Reader.

PAGE 5. It was the City of Westminster travelling library, a large removal-like van parked next to the bins outside one of the kitchen doors. This wasn't a part of the palace she saw much of, and she had certainly never seen the library there before, nor presumably had the dogs, hence the din, so having failed in her attempt to calm them down she went up the little steps of the van in order to apologise.

PAGE 7. 'Is one allowed to borrow a book? One doesn't have a ticket?'
'No problem,' said Mr Hutchings.
'One is a pensioner,' said the Queen, not that she was sure that made any difference.

'Ma'am can borrow up to six books.'
'Six? Heavens!'

PAGE 13. She hadn't really intended to take out another book, but decided that now she was there it was perhaps easier to do it than not, though, regarding what book to choose, she felt as baffled as she had done the previous week.

PAGE 18. What a find Norman was ... Norman was himself and seemed incapable of being anything else ... The Queen, though, might have been less pleased had she known that Norman was unaffected by her because she seemed to him so ancient, her royalty obliterated by her seniority.

PAGE 24. 'Do you know,' she said one afternoon as they were reading in her study, 'do you know the area in which one would truly excel?'

'No, ma'am?'

'The pub quiz. One has been everywhere, seen everything and though one might have difficulty with pop music and some sport, when it comes to the capital of Zimbabwe, say, or the principal exports of New South Wales, I have it all at my fingertips.'

'And I could do the pop,' said Norman.

'Yes,' said the Queen. 'We would make a good team.

PAGE 30, 31. 'I read, I think' she said to Norman, 'because one has a duty to find out what people are like,' a trite enough remark of which Norman took not much notice, feeling himself under no such obligation and reading purely for pleasure, not enlightenment, though part of the pleasure was the enlightenment, he could see that. But duty did not come into it.

To someone with the background of the Queen, though, pleasure had always taken second place to duty.

PAGE 32. These doubts and self-questionings, though, were just the beginning. Once she got into her stride it ceased to seem strange to her that she wanted to read, and books, to which she had taken so cautiously, gradually came to be her element.

PAGE 34, 35. It was with some relief that she got back into the coach and reached behind the cushion for her book. It was not there … When they arrived at the palace she had a word with Grant, the young footman in charge, who said that while ma'am had been in the Lords the sniffer dogs had been round and security had confiscated the book. He thought it had probably been exploded.

'Exploded?' said the Queen. 'But it was Anita Brookner.'

The young man, who seemed remarkably undeferential, said security may have thought it was a device.

The Queen said: 'Yes. That is exactly what it is. A book is a device to ignite the imagination.'

PAGE 39. She smiled a wide smile that indicated that the interview was over and when he turned to bow his head at the door she was already back in her book and without looking up simply murmured 'Sir Kevin' and turned the page.

PAGE 41. Mundane though these conversations might be they had the merit of being predictable and above all, brief, affording Her Majesty plenty of opportunities to cut the exchange short. The encounters ran smoothly and to a schedule, the Queen seemed interested and her subjects were seldom at a loss, and that perhaps the most eagerly anticipated conversation of their lives had only amounted to a discussion of the coned-off sections of the M6 hardly mattered. They had met the Queen and she had spoken to them and everyone got away on time.

… So it was only when it became plain that the tongue-tied quotient was increasing and that more and more of her subjects were at a loss when talking to Her Majesty that the staff began to eavesdrop on what was (or was not) being said.

PAGE 42. Off duty, Piers, Tristram, Giles and Elspeth, all the Queen's devoted servants, compare notes: 'What are you reading? I mean, what sort of question is that Most people, poor dears, aren't reading anything. Except if they say that, madam roots in her handbag, fetches out some volume she's just finished and makes them a present of it.'

'Which they promptly sell on eBay.'

PAGE 44. There were many who hoped for a similar meeting of the minds by saying they were reading Harry Potter, but to this the Queen (who had no time for fantasy) invariably said briskly, 'Yes. One is saving that for a rainy day,' and passed swiftly on.

PAGE 48. At her age, people thought, why bother? To her, though, nothing could be more serious, and she felt about reading what some writers felt about writing, that it was impossible not to do it and that at this late stage of her life, she had been chosen to read as others were chosen to write.

PAGE 53. It was exciting to be with writers she had come to think of as her friends and whom she longed to know. But now ... she found she had nothing to say. She, who had seldom in her life been intimidated by anyone, now found herself tongue-tied and awkward ... Hard put for conversation, she found herself falling back on some of her stock stand-bys. It wasn't quite 'How far have you come?' but their literary equivalent. 'How do you think of your characters? Do you work regular hours? Do you use a word processor?' - questions which she knew were clichés and were embarrassing to inflict had the awkward silence not been worse.

PAGE 60. ... she began her Christmas broadcast with the opening paragraph of **A Tale of Two Cities** ('It was the best of times, it was the worst of times') and it did well, too. Choosing to read not from the autocue but from the book itself, she reminded the older ones in her audience (and they were the majority) of the kind of teacher some could still remember and who had read to them in school.

PAGE 68, 69. ... the tour [to Canada] ... turned out to be disastrous. The Queen was bored, uncooperative and glum, shortcomings all of which her equerries would readily have blamed on her reading, were it not for the fact that, on this occasion, she had no reading. The books Norman had packed for her having unaccountably gone missing ...

... In the far north what few polar bears could be assembled hung about waiting for Her Majesty, but when she did not appear loped off to an ice floe that held more promise.

'Don't you want to look at the St Lawrence Seaway?' said her husband.

'I opened it fifty years ago. I don't suppose it's changed.'

PAGE 72. If Norman didn't know who had engineered his departure, the Queen herself was in no doubt. Norman had gone the way of the travelling library and the case of books that ended up in Calgary. Like the book she had hidden behind the cushion in the state coach, he was lucky not to have been exploded. And she missed him, there was no doubt. But no letter came, no note, and there was nothing for it but grimly to go on. It wouldn't put a stop to her reading.

PAGE 73. People died, people left and (more and more) people got into the papers. For her they were all departures of one sort or another. They left but she went on.

... before Norman's mysterious departure the Queen had begun to wonder if she was outgrowing him ... or rather, out-reading him.

PAGE 78, 79. The household ... went on, running as smoothly as it always did ... It was a ritual of departure and arrival in which she was just a piece of luggage; the most important piece, there was no disputing that, but luggage nevertheless.

In one respect these peregrinations went better than they had done in the past, in that the personage around whom they revolved generally had her nose in a book ... It all made her a pliant and undemanding traveller.

PAGE 88. This time Iran came up and she asked [the prime minister] if he knew of the history of Persia, or Iran (he had scarcely even connected the two), and gave him a book on that besides, and generally began to take such an interest that after two or three sessions like this, Tuesday evenings, which he had hitherto looked forward to as a restful oasis in his week, now became fraught with apprehension.

PAGE 92. 'Reading?' said Sir Claude. 'No harm in that, surely? Her Majesty takes after her namesake, the first Elizabeth. She was an avid reader. Of course, there were fewer books then. And Queen Elizabeth, the Queen Mother, she liked a book. Queen Mary didn't, of course. Or George V. He was a great stamp collector. That's how I started, you know. Licking things.'

PAGE 105. She found ... that when she had written something down, even if it was just an entry in her notebook, she was happy as once she would have been happy after doing some reading. And it came to her again that she did not want simply to be a reader. A reader was next door to being a spectator whereas when she was writing she was doing, and doing was her duty.

PAGE 115. 'A book, Your Majesty. Oh yes, yes. Reminiscences of your childhood, ma'am, and the war, the bombing of the palace, your time in the WAAF.'

'The ATS,' corrected the Queen.

'The armed forces, whatever,' the prime minister galloped on. 'Then your marriage, the dramatic circumstances in which you learned you were Queen. It will be sensational. And,' he chortled, 'there's not much doubt that it will be a bestseller.'

'The bestseller,' trumped the home secretary. 'All over the world.'

'Ye-es,' said the Queen, 'only' – and she relished the moment – 'that isn't quite the kind of book one had in mind. That is a book, after all, that anyone can write and several people have – all of them, to my mind, tedious in the extreme.

PAGE 118. ... 'books, as I'm sure you know, seldom prompt a course of action. Books generally just confirm you in what you have, perhaps unwittingly, decided to do already. You go to a book to have your convictions corroborated. A book, as it were, closes the book.'

PAGE 123, 124. ' ... there was my uncle the Duke of Windsor. He wrote a book, **A King's Story**, the history of his marriage and subsequent adventures ... 'Yes, ma'am ... but the difference, surely, is that His Royal Highness wrote the book as Duke of Windsor. He could only write it because he had abdicated.'

'Oh, did I not say that?' said the Queen. 'But ... why do you think you're all here?'

ACKNOWLEDGEMENTS

ACKNOWLEDGEMENTS

BBC News. "Alan Bennett Reveals Cancer Fight." http://news.bbc.co.uk. September 24, 2005.

Bell, Douglas. "Her Majesty at the Library." The Globe and Mail, Toronto. December 22, 2007.

Bradbury, Malcolm, general editor. **The Atlas of Literature**. Stewart, Tabori and Chang, New York, 1998.

Calhoun, Dave. "Alan Bennett." Time Out Interview. www.timeout.com

Dudding, Adam. "Of Queens and Authors." The Sunday Star Times, New Zealand. December 4, 2007.

Edemariam, Aida. "The Guardian Profile: Alan Bennett." The Guardian, London. Mary 14, 2004

Ellison, Ben. "I Just Want It To Be There." **The Royalist**, October 4, 2006. www.the royalist.net.

Favorite Books of Famous People. Westdale Juniors. 1999. http://www.westdalejuniors.co.uk/spec/favbk.html#RF

Lloyd, John. "An Intellectual in Power." Prospect Magazine, July 2007.

Lyall, Sarah. "Alan Bennett, author of 'The History Boys' speaks out about, of all things, himself." April 16, 2006, London. www.nytimes.com

McCarter, Jeremy. "Ruined by a Book." Sunday New York Times, New York. September 30, 2007.

Miller, Laure. "Barack by the Books." Salon.com, July 7, 2008.

Renzetti, Elizabeth. "The Queen and I." Globe and Mail, Toronto. June 16, 2008.

Rove, Karl. "Bush is a Book Lover." Wall Street Journal, New York. December 26, 2008.